BOOK ANALYSIS

By Candice Kent

Parade's End
by Ford Madox Ford

FORD MADDOX FORD

ENGLISH NOVELIST, POET AND EDITOR

- **Born in Surrey in 1873.**
- **Died in Deauville in 1939.**
- **Notable works:**
  - *The Inheritors* (1901), novel (cowritten with Joseph Conrad)
  - *Fifth Queen* (1906-1908), historical novel trilogy
  - *The Good Soldier* (1915), novel

Ford Maddox Ford, formerly Ford Maddox Heuffer, had parents with both artistic and musical connections. As a consequence, he grew up surrounded by the intellectual and cultural elite of his time. Ford eloped with Elsie Martindale in 1894, but suffered a breakdown from stress caused by the disintegration of his relationship with his wife, aggravated by financial difficulties, in 1904. Following a relationship with the writer, Violet Hunt, Ford departed for France, where he lived with the painter Stella Bowen. After World War I he changed his last name from the German, Heuffer, to Ford.

Throughout his life Ford was a prolific writer of novels, poetry and criticism, as well as editor of the *English Review*. *The Good Soldier* is considered his finest work. It is notable for its use of flash-backs and of an unreliable narrator. Furthermore, his novel tetralogy *Parade's End* continues to be admired for its portrayal of World War I.

PARADE'S END

NOVEL TETRALOGY

- **Genre:** novel
- **Reference edition:** Ford, F. M. (2013) *Parade's End*. Ware: Wordsworth Classics.
- **1st edition:** 1924-1928
- **Themes:** World War I, society, infidelity, divorce, sibling relationships

Parade's End begins several years prior to the start of World War I and concludes several years after the Armistice. The four novels narrate the experiences of Christopher Tietjens, with the events of the first novel, *Some Do Not*, taking place before the war; the events of the second and third novels, *No More Parades* and *A Man Could Stand Up,* taking place during the war; and the concluding novel, *Last Post*, taking place in the post-war years. The novels are presented from the perspectives of various characters and are concerned with Christopher's relationships: primarily with his wife, Sylvia; his brother, Mark; and the woman he loves, Valentine. The debates on morality, principle and pragmatism which pervade the tetralogy reflect the loss of social and moral stability felt in the early part of the 20th century. *Parade's End* is considered a seminal work of fiction set within the context of World War I. It also displays elements of avant-garde literary modernism.

SUMMARY

SOME DO NOT (1924)

The novel begins in 1912 with a description of two young men, government employees, in a railway carriage. The friends are travelling to the country for the weekend. One of the young men is Christopher Tietjens, the novel's protagonist; the other is his friend Vincent Macmaster. Christopher is a gifted mathematician born into the landowning class. He is married and has a child, but his wife, Sylvia, has run off to France with her lover. Macmaster comes from a poor Scottish family. He has ambitions to be a literary critic: indeed, he has just published his first book, and he moves in fashionable artistic circles.

During the course of the weekend Macmaster falls in love with and begins an affair with the wife of the Rev. Mr Duchemin. Simultaneously, Christopher falls in love with the suffragette Valentine Wannop. Although his love is reciprocated, they do not begin a romantic relationship.

Several years later, serving in France during World War I, Tietjens suffers from shell-shock and amnesia. He returns home and lives unhappily with Sylvia, who incorrectly suspects him of having an affair with Valentine. Christopher sees Valentine's mother, Mrs Wannop, frequently, but he seldom meets Valentine, who is busy with her work as a school gym instructor.

Sylvia claims that reports of Tietjens's debauchery have caused his father's death. Christopher's older brother, Mark, visits, and Christopher is able defend himself against the malicious rumours that have been relayed, via his brother, to his father. The brothers are reconciled with the help of Valentine.

As his memory recovers, Tietjens rejects an opportunity to stay in England and opts instead to return to France, where it is very likely he will die.

NO MORE PARADES (1925)

As an army captain in France, Christopher is attempting to send his troops to the front. He faces various obstacles, including insufficient supplies due to corruption; inconsistent orders from his superiors; and a railway strike.

Two of Christopher's men have marital problems. One is the shell-shocked Captain McKechnie, who is in the process of divorcing. The other is a soldier named O Nine Morgan, who wishes to return home to deal with his unfaithful wife. Christopher denies him leave in the fear that his wife's lover will murder him. However, when the base camp is shelled by German fighter craft, O Nine Morgan is killed by shrapnel. Although the marital problems of his men lead Christopher to brood on his own difficulties, he is unwilling to discuss them openly.

Prior to his departure, Sylvia leaves him to go to a convent. He takes this gesture as a sign that their marriage is over and that he is free to become involved with Valentine. However, Sylvia follows Christopher to France and arrives at his camp.

In the early hours of the morning, Christopher throws Sylvia's lover, Perowne, out of her room, and is involved in an altercation with a General O'Hara, who has been attracted by Sylvia's flirting. O'Hara arrests Christopher, but he is released by his godfather, General Campion, and chooses to leave for the front, rather than undergo a court martial, which would expose

Sylvia. In spite of all the distractions and obstacles, Christopher has continued to carry on his administrative duties thoroughly.

A MAN COULD STAND UP (1926)

The third novel in the tetralogy begins with Valentine receiving a telephone call from Lady Macmaster, formerly Mrs Duchemin. Valentine struggles to hear because of the noisy Armistice Day celebrations. Lady Macmaster informs her that Christopher is in London and requires her assistance. She has also, in an earlier conversation, insinuated to the Head of the school that Valentine and Christopher are romantically involved. Valentine decides to commit to Christopher regardless of the consequences.

The focus then shifts to Christopher and to the war at the front earlier in the year. As the bombardments continue, Christopher continues to function effectively in spite of the constant difficulties he faces and in spite of his own fears for his mental health. His thoughts frequently turn to Valentine, so that even a young, blonde soldier reminds him of her. He reflects on his future and decides that once the war is over, he will shake off previous impediments to his relationship with Valentine.

Returning to England and the present, the story resumes with Mrs Wannop attempting unsuccessfully to dissuade Valentine and Christopher from having an affair. Valentine goes to meet Christopher, who also receives visits from his former colleagues from the front. A celebration ensues.

LAST POST (1928)

Mark reflects on the events of the past. Through his memories, the reader discovers what ensues on the night of the Armistice after the close of the third novel. Later on, Valentine's recollection of the same events adds further depth of understanding.

On the night of the Armistice celebrations, Sylvia visits Christopher and announces that she has cancer, and then fakes a fall down the stairs. Valentine dissuades Christopher from believing her. Sylvia publicly accuses Christopher and Valentine of throwing her down the stairs.

Christopher arrives at Mark's home on the eve of the Armistice. He is with Valentine, who is visibly distressed, and announces that they plan to live together. Mark attempts to persuade Christopher to accept Groby manor and its living, so that he might keep himself and Valentine in comfort. Christopher refuses and insists on supporting them both by running an antique furniture business with an American partner.

After learning of the terms of the Armistice, especially that the Allies will not occupy Germany, Mark has a stroke. His wife, and former mistress, Marie Léonie, suspects that he has deliberately withdrawn from the world. As the novel draws to a close, it appears that there may be some truth in her conjecture, although Mark's death at the end undercuts this interpretation.

Christopher has a windfall from an earlier investment and is able to purchase a cottage and lands in beautiful surroundings. Mark and Marie Léonie live with Christopher and Valentine, and the rent they pay, as well as Marie Léonie's efficient management of the home and farm, improve the pair's financial standing. Nevertheless, the pregnant Valentine remains concerned about money. Although she lives frugally, in line with Christopher's principles, she does long for certain small indulgences.

In an effort to hurt Christopher, Sylvia contrives to cut down the great and ancient tree that stands before Groby manor. Although she is successful in this endeavour, Sylvia realises that the tide of sentiment, formerly in her favour, is now shifting towards sympathy for Valentine and Christopher.

CHARACTER STUDY

CHRISTOPHER TIETJENS

The protagonist is a young man belonging to a wealthy and established Yorkshire family with a grand estate named Groby. He is a large, overweight man who takes little care in his dress. He is frequently described as a meal sack, and his lover, Valentine, refers to him as a bear. In spite of the adversity he faces in all areas of his life, he retains his integrity. He is estranged from his unfaithful socialite wife, Sylvia, but he will not disgrace Sylvia by divorcing her. His gallantry toward women is displayed in his first encounter with Valentine when, whilst playing golf with some acquaintances, the game is disrupted by Valentine and another woman as they mount a suffragette protest. Christopher discreetly saves the women from a potentially violent attack by a pair of men, and then from being apprehended by a pursuing policeman.

VINCENT MACMASTER

Christopher's friend is of Scottish birth. His parents are not wealthy and he receives financial support from Christopher and Christopher's parents, who also open doors for him socially, thereby facilitating connections that enable him to rise in government service.

He begins an affair with the wife of the Rev. Duchemin, a parson with whom he had initially made contact with in order to further his literary research.

Mrs Duchemin's husband dies, and she marries Macmaster in secret. Macmaster is successful both in literary circles and in his professional life. He is awarded a knighthood on the strength of work done by Tietjens, whom he fails to credit.

SYLVIA TIETJENS

Christopher's cunning and promiscuous wife, Sylvia, is bored with Christopher's stoical nature and frustrated by his incommunicativeness and his reserve in the face of her betrayals. Sylvia is tall and slim with masses of reddish-blonde hair. Her striking beauty and her flirtatious nature ensure that she is the object of much male attention. She antagonises her husband at every opportunity, and is almost always at the bottom of his troubles. For example, one of her admirers embarrasses Tietjens by unfairly dishonouring his cheques. As seen through the eyes of Christopher's friend, Macmaster, and most especially his brother, Mark, Sylvia is without redeeming qualities and near impossible to sympathise with.

However, when her point of view is explored, in particular in the final novel, one finds that she has limits, which include her reluctance to harm Valentine's unborn child, and that she would have liked to have another child herself. Indeed, Valentine spies her in tears in a moment of discomposure, and discerns in her traces of a kindly nature.

Sylvia's private reflections, if they are accurate, also suggest that the upright Christopher has dubious elements to his morality, based as it is on unfeeling rationality, for example, his view that "defective" children should be euthanised. She is exasperated by her inability to defeat him in arguments on such points, which she considers immoral, and this forms the basis for her suggesting to others that he has an immoral nature.

EDITH ETHEL DUCHEMIN/LADY MACMASTER

Initially the wife of Mr Duchemin, a parson who suffers from bouts of mental illness, Mrs Duchemin is drawn to Macmaster when he succeeds in subduing the parson during one of his bouts, and the two begin an affair. Initially Valentine considers Edith Ethel a friend. This changes when Valentine witnesses Edith Ethel's hostility to Christopher, which is most strikingly obvious when she makes friendly overtures towards Sylvia.

Edith Ethel is ultimately self-serving. When, on Armistice Day, she telephones Sylvia to tell her about Christopher's poor financial and mental state, she is hoping that if she brings Valentine and Christopher together, Valentine will persuade Christopher not to claim back the huge sums of money he has lent Macmaster.

VALENTINE WANNOP

The suffragette, Valentine, loves and is loved by Christopher. She works at a girls' public school but would prefer to have her leisure to read stimulating intellectual matter. She is athletic, petite and blonde.

Valentine is the daughter of an eminent Oxford scholar, who was a close friend of Christopher's father. When her father died, he left Valentine and her mother in dire financial circumstances. Valentine had to support herself and her mother by working as a servant for several months until Christopher's father stepped in to assist Mrs Wannop.

MARK TIETJENS

Christopher's older brother and heir to the Groby estate is initially misled by rumours into believing that Christopher has been living an immoral life and even profiting off the prostitution of his wife. Although the estate is left entirely to Mark, old Mr Tietjens does instruct his oldest son to supply his younger brother with funds when necessary. Despite his efforts, Mark never succeeds in persuading Christopher to accept any financial help.

Mark marries his long-term mistress, Marie Léonie, originally a French dancer, when he fears he is dying of pneumonia. His last words to Marie Léonie, before he is paralysed by a stroke, are a request that she be kind to Valentine. In spite of being unable to speak, his thoughts dominate the narrative of the final novel.

ANALYSIS

NARRATION

When an author tells a story, he or she has to select a point of view from which the account of events and descriptions of characters is given. This is referred to as the narrative mode of the fictional work, and is one of the key factors to consider in the analysis of a novel. The most commonly used modes of narration are third person and first person narratives. In *Parade's End*, Ford Maddox Ford chooses to use the third person narrative form. In contrast to a first person narrator, this type of narrator is outside the story. In a first person narrative, the speaker refers to themselves as 'I' and participates in the events related, such as in Ford's earlier novel, *The Good Soldier*.

A third person narrator is frequently omniscient. According to convention, an omniscient narrator possesses all the necessary knowledge about the events of the novel, unlike the limited first person narrator. The omniscient third person narrator is also privy to the mental and emotional processes of the characters, again unlike the limited first person narrator. Thus, the narrator of *Parade's End* offers us access to the characters' thoughts and feelings.

This narrator may also be intrusive, in the sense that he or she is not restricted to mere reporting, but guides us in our evaluation of the characters' motives, their perspectives on life and their personal qualities. This is the case, for example, in the fiction of the eminent Victorian novelist, George Eliot. Eliot's narrators use the events and the characters as a point of departure for more general observations about life. The narrator of *Parade's End* is, however, unobtrusive. Although the novel begins clearly in the voice of the third person narrator, he or she is, in fact, barely detectable for most of the work. By the end of the first paragraph the voice has already shifted into the thoughts of the protagonist, Christopher. Throughout the novel the narrative voice shifts alternately into the different perspectives of the main characters. The narrative is characterised by extended episodes of introspection which provide a detailed record of thoughts as they pass through the mind of the characters.

Typically, and according to convention, the omniscient narrator's account and judgements are accepted as authoritative. However, the third person narrator is such a diminished presence in *Parade's End*, so that the narrative is dominated by a variety of, often contradictory, points of view as each of the characters comes into focus. There is, therefore, no distinct authoritative account.

MODERNISM

Modernism is generally considered to have been a cultural movement prominent in the early part of the 20th century. In particular the movement reflects responses to the anarchy and futility of World War I and is characterised by a sense that traditional forms were no longer adequate modes of representation. Modernist authors therefore experimented with subject matter and with the formal properties of literature.

One of the characteristics of modernist prose is a disrupted or disjointed narrative. To some extent this can be argued to be a quality of the narrative of *Parade's End*, which consists of various points of view and is, at times, modified by retrospective reflection. For example, in the last novel of the tetralogy, Mark contemplates, among other things, the circumstances of his nephew's birth. He assumes that the younger Mark is the child of another man. However, when he comes face to face with the young man he discovers in him indisputable signs that he is Christopher's son, both in terms of physical characteristics and in terms of mannerisms. He also revises his assumption that his father committed suicide. He had suspected that his father may have had an affair with his closest friend's wife, Mrs Wannop, and that Valentine was therefore Christopher's half-sister. The knowledge of Christopher's relationship with Valentine, Mark believes, drove him to take his own life. As the tetralogy draws to a conclusion, Mark comes to think, instead, that his father was most likely the victim of his own carelessness with his hunting gun. Mark gives no explanation for his revised view on this matter. The reader is left to discover his or her own justifications, through interpretations of the reactions of other characters, such as Mrs Wannop; or to invent justifications; or, indeed, to disagree with Mark's conclusion. Thus, the reader is required to assemble various components of the narrative into an account, and thereby to participate in creating the meaning of the text. This is another trait common to modernist works.

Nevertheless, in novels such as Virginia Woolf's *Mrs Dalloway* (1925), one of the seminal works of modernist literature, which deals with the aftermath of World War I, and in particular with the war's effects on the shell-shocked soldier, one finds a more sustained and intense version of the abovementioned traits. *Parade's End* may, therefore, be argued to straddle traditional Edwardian and experimental modernist modes of representation.

EDWARDIAN SOCIETY

Modernism interrogated the certainties that underpinned traditional modes of morality, religion, social organisation, and conceptions of self. Post-World War I authors felt that previous assumptions regarding the soundness and durability of Western social order needed to be rejected if they were to depict contemporary society with accuracy.

In *Parade's End*, Ford offers a critique of the social mores of his time. For example, the difficulty and disgrace of divorcing is a source of great suffering to Christopher, and to Valentine in particular, who must remain in the degraded position, as it was seen at the time, of mistress, rather than as a socially acceptable and financially secure wife. Ford, furthermore, thereby illustrates another issue: the growing dissatisfaction with the unequal position of women.

Christopher is the model of the traditionally restrained and emotionally self-contained English gentleman. Although his pride and stoicism are admired by his older brother Mark, for example when Christopher refuses to accept money from him even in his most difficult circumstances, Christopher's inflexible rectitude makes his own life very difficult, in particular when he stands up to those who would make easier, less moral choices. The troubles that Christopher faces suggest that in a polite society, or even society as a whole, the devious and self-serving thrive at the expense of the generous and upright. Valentine and Christopher seek a way of living outside or beyond the restrictions of their society.

Comparing *Parade's End* once again with Woolf's *Mrs Dalloway*, one finds that Woolf's shell-shocked soldier, Septimus Warren Smith, similarly sets himself apart from mainstream society, replete with shortcomings as it is, although in a much more extreme way. Whilst Ford's novel shares some of this disillusionment with social order, it does not share the tragic ending of *Mrs Dalloway*. Instead, *Parade's End* concludes on a more optimistic note, as Mark revises his previously pessimistic assumptions about his nephew's paternity and about Valentine's paternity; and as Sylvia relents and accepts defeat in her efforts to thoroughly discredit Christopher and Valentine. Thus, although the various characters of Ford's novel repeatedly observe that times are changing, there is a sense of continuity, exemplified by the unbroken Tietjens' line. This sense of continuity resists modernist interpretations of futility and dislocation.

FURTHER REFLECTION

SOME QUESTIONS TO THINK ABOUT...

- Which narrative method does Ford employ? What effects does the author achieve with this method of narration, and what are its strengths and limitations?
- To what extent does *Parade's End* exemplify the methods and preoccupations of modernism?
- Which aspects of *Parade's End* resist modernist classification?
- How does the author use memory in the construction of the narrative and what are the effects of telling the story in this manner?
- How does Ford characterise Christopher?
- Consider the novel's treatment of conventional Edwardian society. In which areas does it challenge traditions, and where does it advocate continuity? In what ways is this commentary on society relevant today?
- In what ways does *Parade's End* deal with gender issues?
- How does the reader's response to the various characters shift as the narrative progresses?

We want to hear from you!
Leave a comment on your online library
and share your favourite books on social media!

FURTHER READING

REFERENCE EDITION

- Ford, F. M. (2013) *Parade's End*. Ware: Wordsworth Classics.

REFERENCE STUDIES

- Abrams, M. H. (1999) *A Glossary of Literary Terms*. Fort Worth: Harcourt Brace.

MORE FROM BRIGHTSUMMARIES.COM

- Reading guide – *The Good Soldier* by Ford Madox Ford.

Although the editor makes every effort to
verify the accuracy of the information published,
BrightSummaries.com accepts no responsibility for
the content of this book.

www.brightsummaries.com

Ebook EAN: 9782808019682

Paperback EAN: 9782808019699

Legal Deposit: D/2019/12603/151

Cover: © Primento

Digital conception by Primento, the digital partner of
publishers.